The Juneteenth Drama

Earl Ofari Hutchinson

Copyright 202

Publisher's Cataloging-in-Publication Data

Names: Hutchinson, Earl Ofari. Title: Reparations! / Earl Ofari Hutchinson.
Description: Los Angeles, CA : Middle Passage Press, 2023. | Includes bibliographic
references and index. | Summary: Examines the many facets of the U.S. debate over the
Juneteenth Holiday,

Identifiers: LCCN pending| ISBN 979=8-89074-005-2 (pbk.)

Subjects: LCSH: African Americans -- Juneteenth | Slavery and historical injustices --
United States. | Slavery -- United States -- Public opinion. | Racism -- Political aspects --
United States. | Compensation (Law) -- United States. |

BISAC: SOCIAL SCIENCE / Discrimination. | SOCIAL SCIENCE / Slavery. |
POLITICAL SCIENCE / Civil Rights.

Classification: LCC E185.89.R45 H88 2023 | DDC 323.1196 H--dc22

LC record available at https://lccn.loc.gov/202390874

Table of Contents

Introduction

1.They Didn't Know They Were Free

2 The Juneteenth Battle

3 The Reluctant Holiday

Conclusion

Sources

About the Author

Introduction

In June 2021 Wisconsin GOP Senator Ron Johnson cast one of the most surprising Senate votes recorded in living memory. One year earlier he had virtually single-handedly blocked passage of a bill the House had approved that would have made Juneteenth a federal national holiday. Johnson concocted this convenient rationale for his obstructionism. He said that declaring yet another national holiday would put taxpayers and the Treasury on the hook for gobs of lost tax dollars.

A year later, he didn't exactly sing a different tune. But this time with Senate Minority Leader Mitch McConnell and every other GOP senator solidly on board to declare Juneteenth a national holiday, Johnson caved and voted for the holiday. That made the GOP senators vote unanimous.

This was a bittersweet moment for Juneteenth holiday advocates. For years they had pressed hard to make the day a national holiday. The Senate approval put the final legal stamp on their battle. Juneteenth, long a state holiday in Texas, was the date that Union General Gordon Granger in Texas publicly announced that slavery had formally ended. The announcement was a formality. Lincoln's Emancipation Proclamation issued January 1,

1863, freed all slaves in states in rebellion against the U.S. Texas was one of them.

*****

The fight to make Juneteenth a federal holiday itself was a stirring drama. A drama that was filled with a hearty mix of hope, anger, frustration, mythology, and politics. But above it has been a drama layered with race and the continuing rancor over America's slave past. The Juneteenth federal holiday push stirred a titanic battle to shove, cajole, and browbeat America into facing up to its slave past.

In *the Juneteenth Drama*, political analyst Earl Ofari Hutchinson presents a brief, but concise, assessment of these issues. He contends that the battle for Juneteenth national recognition was a movement that was driven in part by compassion, in part by guilt, and in part by a need to confront painful racial issues. It also was a relatively easy, and cost-free political concession to African Americans. Still, it was the right one for Congress and the country to make. *The Juneteenth Drama* tells that story.

1

They Didn't Know They Were Free!

It was long an inside joke for someone to say that Juneteenth was a testament to ignorance. The ignorance was that slaves in Texas were supposedly too dumb, ignorant, or uninformed, or all three, to realize that two-plus years had passed since they were freed.

President Abraham Lincoln signed the Emancipation Proclamation on January 1, 1863. As of that day, the enslaved in states in rebellion against the United States were technically freed. Yet it supposedly took two more years for enslaved Blacks in Texas to figure that out. This horrible tall tale repeatedly cropped up and became part of the sometimes amusing folklore around Juneteenth. It was just that, folklore, not fact.

A substantial amount of oral history was done with and about slaves in Texas and other states. The former slaves insisted that they were not dumb or hoodwinked about slavery's technical end with Lincoln's proclamation. Felix Haywood, a slave in Texas during the Civil War, in one of the oral history interviews debunked the myth of slave ignorance, "We knowed what was goin' on in [the war] all the time. We all felt like heroes, and nobody had made us that way but ourselves."

*****

The profound importance of Juneteenth began the moment Union Major General Gordon Granger read his proclamation Order #3. The order had absolutely nothing to do with informing the former slaves that they were now free. The order spelled out the labor, social, and property rights, of Blacks as well as the place of free Blacks within white society.

Granger specified that the order guaranteed "absolute equality of personal rights and rights of property between former masters and slaves." It further clarified the relationship between slaveholders and the formerly enslaved as one "between employer and hired labor."

Granger's other great concern was to make clear what the Union troops and the government were prepared to do to assist the freedmen. As it turned out very little. In fact, Granger was blunt. They would have to work for wages, and in doing so "idleness" would not be tolerated, let alone subsidized.

The former enslaved knew this. The former slave masters knew this too. Texas newspapers ran countless stories and editorials mostly denouncing Lincoln's Emancipation Proclamation as well as Granger's order. That ensured that the order would be widely if not incessantly discussed by whites, especially the slave masters. The formerly enslaved

Blacks and the many free Blacks did much to spread the word about the new order of race relations.

"There was an incredibly sophisticated communication network among slaves in Texas," noted Edward T. Cotham, Jr., Texas Civil War historian and author of *Juneteenth, The Story Behind The Celebration,* "News like that spread like wildfire. We know some slaves knew about the Emancipation Proclamation even before slaveowners. It didn't mean anything because there was no army to enforce it."

An African American direct descendant in Galveston of a slave family confirmed this, "It wasn't that all these poor people didn't get the message," she observed, "It was that there was no one enforcing it, no one making it happen!"

*****

There was yet another reason Graham had to spell out in harsh and forceful terms the end of slavery. Texas slaveholders and most whites in the state bitterly resisted slavery's end. They tried every subterfuge from murder and naked terror to even trying to continue to buy and sell slaves. Every stop was pulled out to keep alive the near-dead institution.

The counter was a massive show of force by the Union army and federal officials. They needed the support of the former slaves to finally force the former slave masters to capitulate. To secure that they imposed a code of relations and a guideline on the status of the Blacks. The key element was that the Blacks had to be reassured that they were truly free laborers with full civil rights, and the legal right to own property.

Granger's order, then, was a pragmatic tact to ensure stability, control, and the rule of law. One historian observed, "It's not that General Granger was giving information to the enslaved people. He was giving it to the masters."

The order, though, wasn't the magic tonic to force compliance. The estimate is that four hundred Blacks were murdered between 1865 and 1868. The terror was designed to intimidate the former slaves. The death toll was almost certainly far higher.

There was yet another reason for the seeming lag in the Texas slaveholder's capitulation to emancipation. Texas was a well-established dumping ground slaveholders in other states such as Mississippi and Alabama used to move their slave property to. The aim was to put as much distance as possible from the Union army and officials who sought to implement emancipation. Texas was ideal for that purpose.

It was on the far periphery of the South's slaveocracy. It was still largely frontier, and transportation and communication were primitive to non-existent in many parts of the state. Therefore, it was simply convenient to use Texas as a fail-safe area to maintain slavery as long as possible after its formal end. Granger's added aim, then, with the issuance of the order was to break the back of the last bastion of the slaveocracy. Thus, it took a

special measure, General Order #3, to drive that point forcefully
home not to the slaves, but their enslaver captors

2

The Juneteenth Battle

There was no surprise that more than a dozen Republican House members in June 2021, said no to the bill that came as close to being unanimous as possible in getting agreement between the GOP and Democrats on a bill. The final vote on the bill to make Juneteenth a federal holiday as expected passed overwhelmingly. That is except for the fourteen GOP House members that voted against it.

The GOP opponents were careful to give the public impression that race, and racism, had nothing to do with their no vote. They masked their opposition to it with the claim that the bill's name—National Independence Day was wrong-headed and misleading. There was only one National Independence Day the country should honor. That was July 4th. Labeling Juneteenth with that name, they argued, would confuse too many people, and minimize the importance of July 4 in the nation's history.

But race lurked near the surface. Kentucky congressman Tom Massie who voted no unsheathed the racial mask, "I fully support creating a day to celebrate the abolition of slavery, a dark portion of our nation's history. However, naming this day 'National Independence Day' will create confusion and push Americans to pick one of those two days as their Independence Day based on their racial identity."

Several of the other fourteen GOP opponents were even coarser on race. They charged that the holiday would create more racial division and even worse, it was just another effort to cram critical race theory down America's throats.

They did not explain just how a holiday that celebrated freedom and directly confronted America's hideous slave legacy would create racial discord. But then again, they didn't have to.

*****

For decades, many African American advocacy groups, civil rights organizations, political officials, and scores of genealogical societies had vigorously pushed for making Juneteenth a national holiday. In each case, they met the same wall of race-leaden arguments against it.

During most of those years, the issue largely flew under the media and the public's radar scope. That changed in 2018. Then a loose group dubbed the Juneteenth Movement kicked the campaign for a federal holiday into high gear.

It organized marches, demonstrations, and walks in various cities, including Washington D.C., to press Congress to act. The group collected more than a million and a half signatures on a petition to federalize the day.

The movement had a ready congressional precedent to point to make the case for the federal holiday.

Twenty years earlier in April 1997, the Senate passed a resolution, sponsored ironically by hard-core conservative Mississippi senator Trent Lott. The resolution "commemorated Juneteenth as Independence Day." In calling it Independence Day the resolution established the name template for Juneteenth. The resolution passed unanimously.

The resolution was a fairly easy concession to make. It required no action. The Congressional Budget Office estimated the cost to taxpayers at zero dollars. It was a case of textbook feel-good racial political symbolism over substance.

*****

There was yet one more irony in the GOP's effort to stonewall a Juneteenth federal holiday. Then President Donald Trump supplied it. The day before the Juneteenth celebration in June 2020, he waded into the Juneteenth controversy. He had scheduled a campaign rally in Tulsa, Oklahoma on June 19.

Howls immediately went up that Trump was practically desecrating the day by holding his rally that day. Trump heard the howls of protest and in characteristic Trump fashion tried mightily to turn the tables. He pushed the rally back a day to June 20.

In pure Trump theater of the absurd, he took full credit for putting Juneteenth on the national radar scope. Said Trump, "I did something good: I made Juneteenth very famous. It's actually an important event, an important time. But nobody had ever heard of it."

There was both truth and fiction in Trump's retort. Tennessee in 2023 still had special days honoring Confederate traitors Robert E. Lee and Nathan Bedford Forrest. Yet, the GOP-controlled state legislature was one of several Deep South states that said no to making Juneteenth a paid holiday for state workers in 2022.

It masked the opposition with the claim that almost no one knew anything about it, "I asked many people in my district over the last few days, well over 100 people, if they knew what Juneteenth was and only two of them knew," said Republican Sen. Joey Hensley, who is white and voted against the proposal. "I just think we're putting the cart before the horse making a holiday that people don't know about."

As further proof of this, Trump claimed that he polled a lot of people on it, and not one of them had heard of Juneteenth. Maybe Trump had suffered a convenient temporary memory lapse about it. An aide reminded him that he had issued a statement the year before commemorating the date. Trump had a fallback answer to his ignorance, "Oh, really? We put out a statement? The Trump White House put out a statement?" He quickly added that that was "good."

Trump couldn't let the lapse go and gave some credit to an African American Secret Service agent. He said he filled him in on the importance of the day.

Trump continued to sniff political gain by posing as the champion of Juneteenth. Three months later at a campaign rally in Atlanta with his eye on trying to peel off a few Black votes from Biden, he boasted that he'd push hard to make Juneteenth a federal holiday. He didn't say how or give any timetable for making the push.

*****

But then again, he didn't have to. It was enough for him to pledge, hoping as always that it might at least get the eye and ear of some Black voters in a state, Georgia, which was rated a toss-up in the 2020 presidential election. Black voters there almost certainly would make a difference in helping to sink his candidacy in the state.

Still, Trump posing as the champion of Juneteenth was almost laughable. But it was Trump, so anything he said or did to further Trump was never a surprise. Juneteenth is just one of many examples.

Trump's braggadocio about taking credit for Juneteenth's popularity and his pledge to make it a federal holiday notwithstanding things had sharply changed when the bill was close to passage. The right had drummed up the canard of critical race theory as the hidden agenda behind Juneteenth. It sought to use the issue to rally, mobilize, and inflame the GOP's core base voters. So, shoving Juneteenth into the mix on that issue simply made good political talking points for the right.

*****

The other issue that was in part a strawman, and in part a standard concern for fiscal conservatives was the cost of adding another federally designated holiday to the calendar. This was not the first time that conservatives raised this objection to the creation of a federal holiday. It was a sticking point in the fight over the federal holiday for Dr. Martin Luther King Jr. in the 1980s. That debate, like Juneteenth, was layered with overt racial controversy. The figure repeatedly tossed out for the King federal holiday was $660 million in lost payroll, wages, and tax revenues.

This delayed but ultimately did not stop a reluctant then-President Ronald Reagan from signing the King Holiday bill into law in 1983. Even as the Juneteenth bill garnered the massive bi-partisan support it did for passage, which didn't stop opponents from raising objections about the cost.

Some recycled the ploy that the bill should have been tossed back to the CBO for study on the cost of the holiday. Texas congressperson Sheila Jackson waved off the ploy, "I don't think that we will lose our shirt by adding only one other holiday that commemorates the life, the legacy, and the history of African Americans."

Of course, Jackson and other Juneteenth holiday backers knew that the issue was never about any potential revenue loss. The GOP never raised any objection to profligate, wasteful and unnecessary spending on the mammoth, and grotesque military weaponry budget. Nor did it raise objections to other endless wasteful high-cost pork barrel projects and spending measures in their congressional districts. In almost all cases, these projects feathered the profit nests of businesses and especially corporations. The issue, as always, was race, and hard-core cutthroat partisan politics.

The hard right remained relentlessly obsessed with anything real and imagined it could tie into the assault on critical race theory, or its companion buzz words, identity politics. The point was to try and startle and convince conservative whites that the radical left was trying to use racial issues to sow guilt among whites. One of the House Republicans who said no to the Juneteenth holiday bill didn't try to hide this.

Montana GOP Representative Matt Rosendale lambasted the Juneteenth movement and the holiday as nothing more than another effort to "create a day out of whole cloth to celebrate identity politics," all with the end goal of pushing critical race theory on the nation's precious white population. He added in case the point was missed "Let's call an ace an ace," "The Left has made up what was primarily a Texas holiday, which they are now acting like they recently discovered, in order to continually make Americans feel bad and convince them that our country is evil."

"This isn't an effort to commemorate emancipation," he continued. "It's very clearly tied to the larger hard-left agenda to enshrine the racial history of this country as the prime aspect of our national story."

Rosendale at least was honest. He didn't hide behind the canards of cost and an objection to the name. Though most of the House Republicans backed the Juneteenth bill as well as all the GOP Senators, this was no real signal that the GOP and hard rightists had in any way had an epiphany of political enlightenment. It was simply the least costly financial and political way to confirm its continual refrain that the GOP was not racist. It was just another crude and transparent effort to ward off the relentless and deserved barrage of attacks on the GOP for its chronic racial antagonism.

Nebraska Governor Pete Ricketts left little doubt that the GOP's stripes on race hadn't changed, "The effect of critical race theory is to pit the American people against one another, rather than building a more perfect union that promotes the dignity of all Americans and respect for people of all backgrounds."

Still, Juneteenth, despite the GOP's cynicism, duplicity, and hypocrisy, was a hard battle finally won. It wouldn't and couldn't be taken off the books and the national table.

There was sweet final proof of this. Eight of the GOP obstructionist House members that said no to the Juneteenth federal holiday gave up and closed their offices on the inaugural Juneteenth holiday in June 2021.

19

3
The Reluctant Holiday

One year after Congress passed and President Biden signed into law the bill making Juneteenth a federal holiday, *Gallup* took a poll about the holiday. The majority of Americans had heard of Juneteenth. However, when probed about it a majority knew little to nothing about Juneteenth, its significance, and even why it was declared a federal holiday.

Many of the states took their cue from the public's ignorance about the holiday. Most of the states did not give their employees the day off as a paid holiday day. Most private businesses followed suit. They did not give their employees the day off either.

There was nothing that Congress or the White House could do about that. They did not have the power to compel states to observe a federal holiday. Federal holidays are just that federal holidays. The only employees who are legally entitled to a paid holiday day off are federal employees and those in the District of Columbia.

The issue of who does and doesn't celebrate a federal holiday was a point of sharp contention and controversy in celebrating the King federal holiday from the moment Reagan signed the bill making it a holiday into law in 1983.

*****

For the first two decades, most businesses did not give their employees a paid day off. Most states followed the same pattern. That gradually changed as more states and businesses came on board to acknowledge the holiday with a paid day off for workers. Yet the fierce resistance continued. In 2020, the King Holiday was a workday for more than eighty percent of workers in manufacturing businesses. That remained the case in 2023.

Despite the recognition of the King Holiday as a national holiday by all fifty states, observance of the King Holiday remained largely a discretionary matter for most state officials. The District of Columbia is the only public district that mandates the King holiday as a work-off day for federal employees.

The mixed reaction to the King Holiday ranged from turning a blind eye, indifference, or just outright ignoring it in many quarters. In signing the King holiday bill, Reagan strongly signaled that this was not likely to change, "To make it a national holiday in the sense of businesses closing down and government closing down and everyone not working? I'd like to call your attention to [the fact that] we only really have a couple of those...not even Abraham Lincoln has that kind of a national holiday."

In far too many public and private circles, the King Holiday was regarded as a "Black holiday" or more charitably a "civil rights issue." That reinforced the chronic fiction that King was solely a Black leader, that the civil rights movement was a movement only for Blacks, and that his holiday should be celebrated exclusively by Blacks.

The same tag was inevitably slapped on Juneteenth. That fiction was amply reinforced by pictures of marches, rallies, events, and festivals on that day in which in most instances the marchers and celebrants shown were African Americans.

There's also the question of numbers. The Juneteenth holiday is the eleventh federal holiday. In the century before Juneteenth was added to the federal holiday calendar, only four federal holidays were added. This is a double-edged sword. On the one hand, purely in terms of numbers, there is a scarcity of federal holidays. On the other, some consider that there are too many.

It's a Hobbesian Choice dilemma. The more holidays on a calendar over time diminishes the impact and importance to many Americans of the holiday. It's just another day off for many.

However, a holiday such as the King Holiday and the Juneteenth Holiday were intended as holidays to cajole, educate and remind Americans of America's history of racial turmoil, struggles, and progress. They are not holidays for leisure or shopping. "Juneteenth marks the date of major significance in American history. It represents the ways in which freedom for Black people has been delayed," said Democratic Rep. Anthony Nolan, who fought to make making Juneteenth a paid holiday in Connecticut. He added, "If we delay this, it's a smack in the face to Black folks."

The irony is that GOP state legislators in some of the states where legislators dragged their feet on making Juneteenth an official state holiday, moved with lightning speed to limit what can be taught about systematic racism in classrooms.

They also moved swiftly to introduce and pass bills to scuttle critical race theory teaching even when almost none of the nation's school districts mandated in 2023 that it be taught. They likewise moved speedily to torpedo the expansion of voting rights protections and meaningful police reforms.

Yet, despite the foot-dragging and obstructionism, fifty states in one way or another recognize Juneteenth. That speaks for itself.

Conclusion

The fight to get Juneteenth recognized as a significant event in

American history and to equally recognize the significant imprint it made on American race relations was long, tortuous, and dramatic. It hit many bumps along the way. One was the contention that it was just a local occurrence in one state. Another was that it reflected the ignorance of enslaved Blacks in Texas about emancipation.

Then after the day attained national recognition and the push was on to make it a federal holiday, the opponents rolled out a fresh arsenal of attacks. It was just another effort, they claimed, to reinforce identity politics and shove a New Left agenda of Critical Race Theory down the nation's (i.e. whites) throats.

Then when it got traction within Congress for passage there were new hits. It was unnecessary. That is the country did not need another federal holiday. It was too costly. And it had local significance to one state only Texas.

The final hit point was the name. The opponents screamed long and loud about it being designated Independence Day. They angrily reminded that there was only one American Independence Day. That was July 4th. Naming Juneteenth Independence Day would simply confuse too many people and it was a misnomer.

*****

Fortunately, Congress didn't listen to the opponents. The Senate passed it unanimously. The House did almost the same except for the usual hard-right die-hard suspects. That is fourteen GOP reps who said no to the holiday. The House still passed it by an overwhelming vote.

President Biden quickly signed it into law on June 16, 2021. He aptly noted, "Juneteenth marks both a long, hard night of slavery and subjugation and the promise of a brighter morning to come. This is a day, in my view, of profound weight and profound power, a day in which we remember the moral stain, terrible toll that slavery took on the country and continues to take."

The operative words from Biden were the toll that slavery "continues to take on the country." Juneteenth was a signpost, a bellwether, and a marker that again cast an ugly glare on America's hideous slave past. It also cast it on the legacy of slavery that has resulted in the chronic, gaping racial inequities in education, housing, health care, and the plague of police violence against Blacks.

Juneteenth was never intended to be a panacea for the continuing crushing legacy of slavery. However, it was a tiny and crucial step toward the acknowledgement of a horrid past and present racial wrong. Equally important, it would mark a modest but significant attempt to continue to confront that past.

Sources

Ted Barrett, et.al., "Senate unanimously passes a bill making Juneteenth a federal holiday," *CNN*, June 15, 2021

https://www.cnn.com/2021/06/15/politics/juneteenth-federal-holiday-senate-vote/index.html

John Burnett, "Four enduring myths about Juneteenth are not based on facts," *NPR*, June 20, 2022

https://www.npr.org/2022/06/20/1105945119/four-enduring-myths-about-juneteenth-are-not-based-on-facts

Simmone Shaw, "The Surprisingly Progressive Promises of General

Order No. 3, Which Ended Slavery in Texas," *Time*, June 17, 2022
https://time.com/6188864/general-order-3-juneteenth/

Robin Washington, "Here's What Really Happened on Juneteenth," *Forward,* June 18, 2021

https://forward.com/opinion/471597/juneteenth-what-really-happened/

Gregory P. Downs, "The Hidden History of Juneteenth," *TPM*, June 18,2015

The Hidden History Of Juneteenth - TPM – Talking Points Memo

Maegan Vazquez, "Trump Claims He Deserves credit for making Juneteenth 'very famous,' "*CNN*, June 18,

2020https://www.cnn.com/2020/06/18/politics/donald-trump-juneteenth-credit/index.html

Steve Holland, "Trump Pledges to Make Juneteenth a Federal Holiday in Bid for Black Voters, "*Yahoo News*, September 25, 2020

https://news.yahoo.com/trump-pledges-juneteenth-federal-holiday-203111409.html?fr=sycsrp_catchall

Connor Perrrett, "8 GOP reps who voted against making Juneteenth a

national holiday appeared to close their offices anyway: report," *Insider*,

June 19, 2021

https://www.businessinsider.com/gop-reps-who-voted-against-juneteenth-closed-offices-anyway-2021-6

Eric Lutz, "Republicans Try Justifying Opposition to Juneteenth Holiday: Divisive, Confusing, and Tied to the "Hard-Left Agenda," *Vanity Fair*, June 17, 2021
https://www.vanityfair.com/news/2021/06/republicans-try-justifying-opposition-to-juneteenth-holiday-divisive-confusing-and-tied-to-the-hard-left-agenda

"Companies Making Juneteenth A Paid Holiday Say It's The Right Thing To Do, *NPR*, June 17, 2021 https://www.npr.org/2021/06/17/1007551309/14-house-republicans-voted-against-making-juneteenth-a-federal-holiday

S.J.Res.11 - A joint resolution commemorating "Juneteenth Independence Day," June 19, 1865, the day on which slavery finally came to an end in the United States." *Congress.Gov*, April 14, 1997

https://www.congress.gov/bill/105th-congress/senate-joint-resolution/11

Destinee Adams, "How to properly celebrate Juneteenth in the age of commercialization," *NPR*, June 20,2022

https://www.npr.org/2022/06/20/1106193407/celebrate-juneteenth-the-right-way

Vanessa Romo, "One Woman's Decades-Long Fight To Make Juneteenth A U.S. Holiday," *NPR*, June 17, 2021

https://www.npr.org/2021/06/17/1007498876/how-juneteenth-became-national-holiday

Lauren Egan, "Biden Signs into law a bill establishing Juneteenth as aa federal holiday," *NBC*, June 17, 2021

https://www.nbcnews.com/politics/white-house/biden-signs-law-bill-establishing-juneteenth-federal-holiday-n1271213

"Despite Push, States Slow to Make Juneteenth a Paid Holiday," *US News*, June 15, 2022
https://www.usnews.com/news/politics/articles/2022-06-15/despite-push-states-slow-to-make-juneteenth-a-paid-holiday

About the Author

Earl Ofari Hutchinson is an author and political analyst. He has written extensively on race and politics in America. His latest book, *Mass Shootings-Made in America* (Monthly Review Press). He is the host of the weekly Earl Ofari Hutchinson Show on KPFK-Radio 9 AM Saturdays and the Pacifica Network. He is the publisher of thehutchinsonreport.net